WHEN JESUS CAME TO TOWN

Gina Cronrath

WestBow Press books may be ordered through booksellers or by contacting:

WestBow Press
A Division of Thomas Nelson & Zondervan
1663 Liberty Drive
Bloomington, IN 47403
www.westbowpress.com
844-714-3454

ISBN: 978-1-6642-1620-4 (sc)
ISBN: 978-1-6642-1621-1 (e)

Library of Congress Control Number: 2020924697

Print information available on the last page.

WestBow Press rev. date: 12/18/2020

WESTBOW
PRESS®
A DIVISION OF THOMAS NELSON
& ZONDERVAN

WHEN JESUS
CAME TO TOWN

It was almost Christmas time. The stores were selling toys, mothers were baking cookies, and the air was cold and crisp. Everything seemed the same as every other year, until one day something was different

We heard on the radio, that Santa was coming to the library that afternoon to find out what all of the children wanted for Christmas.

So most of the moms bundled their children up in their warm coats and hats and headed for the library that cold winter afternoon, when Christmas was almost here.

When we got to the library, we didn't see Santa. Instead, we saw a man wearing what looked like a choir robe sitting in a comfortable chair. He looked kind and nice. The librarian told us to line up and we could go talk to him one by one.

So we waited our turn to talk to whoever this was. We still wondered what had happened to Santa.

The kind man told us that Santa was called out of town unexpectedly. He told us his name was Jesus, and He was God's Son. Instead of what toys we wanted, He wanted to know what had made us sad or angry this past year.

Susie told Him that her brothers were always being mean to her by calling her names and hiding her toys. Jesus handed her a small package in the shape of a heart. As she held it in her hand, Susie could feel more love in her heart to give away to her brothers. She even wanted to talk to them in a kind way.

Next, it was my friend, David's turn. He told Jesus, he had been feeling selfish lately and didn't want to share toys or anything else he had with his friends or family. Jesus handed him an empty box. David asked what he was supposed to do with an empty box. This thought came to him all of a sudden. The next time you are feeling selfish, put something you like in this box and give it to someone else. That will make you happier than any toy ever could.

Finally, it was my turn. I went and sat on Jesus's lap in that big comfortable chair. I knew what I needed to say. I hadn't been very helpful to my family or other people lately. My room was messy; I left my clothes on the floor, and didn't help my friends or neighbors much.

Jesus handed me a picture of a pair of hands holding a heart. I knew that this was my heart and Jesus's hands. As I gave Him all of the feelings of not wanting to help others, I was given a heart that couldn't wait to help!

I left the library that day, feeling better. My friends left feeling better, too. This would be the best Christmas ever. Not because we got all of the toys we wanted, but because we got something even more valuable. We had all received the gift of Love from Jesus that would last forever.

Printed in the United States
By Bookmasters